YOUR KNOWLEDGE HAS VALUE

Bibliographic information published by the German National Library:

The German National Library lists this publication in the National Bibliography; detailed bibliographic data are available on the Internet at http://dnb.dnb.de .

Imprint:

Copyright © 2019 GRIN Verlag
Print and binding: Books on Demand GmbH, Norderstedt Germany
ISBN: 9783346034939

This book at GRIN:

https://www.grin.com/document/501264

Iryna Lysenko

The Debate on the Ban on Headscarves in French Schools. A Symbol for the Threatened Unity of the French Republic?

GRIN Verlag

GRIN - Your knowledge has value

Since its foundation in 1998, GRIN has specialized in publishing academic texts by students, college teachers and other academics as e-book and printed book. The website www.grin.com is an ideal platform for presenting term papers, final papers, scientific essays, dissertations and specialist books.

Visit us on the internet:

http://www.grin.com/

http://www.facebook.com/grincom

http://www.twitter.com/grin_com

Iryna Lysenko
Sociology
University Bielefeld
Erasmus Student
Fifth semester   03.06.2019

The debate on the ban on headscarves in French schools.

Contents

Introduction..*3*

Talal Asad`s view of the French secularism *5*

Jansen Yolande`s view of the French secularism..*6*

Comparison of both approaches *6*

Conclusion *7*

Resources *9*

Introduction

For more than twenty years, the Muslim headscarf has regularly raised public debates on the content and values of the French Republic, its relationship to cultural plurality in general and to the Maghreb population of the former colonies in particular. This is the main part of the Muslim minority in France. The headscarf has become a symbol of the threat to secular values and thus to the Republic as such, and is seen as the omen of fundamentalist Islam, incompatible with the democratic-liberal values of France.

From the beginning of 2003 to the beginning of 2004, the discussions about the headscarf in France flared up particularly strongly and provoked passionate internal social controversies that overtook all other national and international debates. Demands for a legal ban on the headscarf became more and more urgent: it was about laicism, preserving the unity of the French Republic, protecting the young Muslim woman from male oppression and thus upholding human rights, halting the advance of a political Islam that was dangerous for the Republic and putting a stop to the resulting "communitarian tendencies". The debates took on a scale that led the government, in the autumn of 2003, to entrust a commission of experts with the task of verifying compliance with the basic principles of secularism in the Republic and, in particular, in French schools. The so-called "Stasi Commission", led by immigration expert Bernard Stasi, drew up a bill after several months of investigation which reaffirmed the general demands to prohibit girls of school age from wearing headscarves in school lessons. In March 2004, a law banning the wearing of ostentatious religious signs in schools and public institutions was passed.

But what actually led to the headscarf debate being able to occupy politics and the media to such an extent, and the Republic seeing itself questioned in its foundations or in the values that constitute them? Can some headscarves worn by minors in schools really threaten the unity of the Republic and the concept of secularism to such an extent that they have to be stopped by law, or are social problems that only remotely have something to do with the actual message of the headscarf worked off against the girls? Is it possible to speak of the headscarf at all, or does it not rather represent a range of meanings from the underlining of ethno-religious descent, traditional habitus to the emphasis on religious identity? Is the headscarf really a sign of female oppression and thus an affront to gender justice anchored in international human rights?

All these questions raised in the course of the social discourse about the headscarf are not necessarily connected, but have been continuously mixed up in the course of the debate. The

3

result was a dense cluster of topics, which was only loosely held together by the scarf and the concept of the headscarf debate itself.

The aim of the present work is to unravel this tangle and to work out the individual themes from which the debate was nourished.

The basic assumption of my work is that the theme of the headscarf and the strands of association linked to this symbol, such as fundamentalist Islam, cultural archaism and female oppression, are instrumentalized for a number of socially relevant secondary discourses, such as the question of the identity of the French Republic in a society that is becoming increasingly pluralistic both religiously and culturally, and the handling of a steadily growing Islamic community in France.

The work is also intended to draw attention to the topic and, for example, to deal in more detail with the gender debate that is developing in subsequent work. This analysis is based on two commentaries, each of which irradiates the headscarf debate differently. In the following chapter Talal Asad comments on the behaviour of the state, because it cannot take the right out of it to determine what religious signs or individual orientation is. The next chapter deals more with assimilation and the problems that arise in this context. It will be discussed to what extent it seems impossible in our modern society to drop habitualized religious symbols. Finally, a comparison of these two approaches and a personal statement on this topic will follow.

One of the motifs of the investigation that runs through all chapters of this work is the question of whether and in what way the headscarf, "alienated" from the girls in the course of the debates, served various public discourses as a legitimate means of distracting attention from the experiences of racism and exclusion of the 2nd and 3rd generations, of working off problems within society, and of strengthening a common, French sense of identity.

Talal Asad's view of the French secularism

In his work Talal Asad deals with the power of the French state. As already mentioned in the introduction, the Stasi report discussed the wearing of headscarves in schools and identified it as an oppression of young women. According to the theory of secularism, religion and politics should be separated. Secularism is reinterpreted by the French state and called Laïcité. In her commentary, Asad has to expose the fact that through this ideology the state evaluates and restricts religions with the law introduced in 2004.

"The headscarf worn by Muslim schoolgirls has become the symbol of many aspects of social and religious life among Muslim immigrants and their offspring to which secularists object" (Asad 2005: 94). The state assumes that the conspicuous religious symbols endanger the morals and social norms of French society. According to Asad, the actual task of the state is to ensure the well-being of the citizens and their security. With its current behaviour, the state segregates between religions and the moral view of politics. This leads to disputes between French politics and its citizens. Multiculturalism puts the state in a complicated position, while France, with its restrictions, tries to guide its citizens towards integration. Thus, Asad demands that the state should first sensitize itself to the religions, so that one gets a better understanding of each religion, in order to construct from it a regulation fair for all parties. Thus, for the first time a definition of religions would be necessary in order to formulate an acceptable standard for all. Thus in 2004 a bill was passed prohibiting the wearing of conspicuous religious symbols in school institutions. In which the state took the power to determine that headscarves are worn voluntarily according to their understanding, which, however, is not the case in the strictly Muslim faith. The French state thus did not understand the asymmetry of the meaning of the headscarf. On the other hand, Asad describes the restriction of freedom of opinion and religion. Asad sees the problem not only in secularism itself, but also in the lack of neutrality towards religions. But why did the French state decide to secularize at all? The reason lies in the history of France and the newly emerging insecurity of politics. Thus, secularism was apparently only expanded in France, since a mistrust towards Muslims developed and no other solution was found.

In conclusion, Asad sees this law as a violation of freedom of expression, and politicians have devised a superficial solution to a cultural problem. However, the Christian religion has always been a component of French politics, so it would be utopian now to separate these two powers completely from the point of view that one is insufficiently informed about the newly appearing religions in the country.

In the next chapter the perspective of Yolande will be dealt with.

Jansen Yolande's view of the French secularism

Jansen Yolande is a professor at the University of Amsterdam. She specializes in multiculturalism and secularization. In addition, she does research at the Amsterdam Centre for Globalisation. Yolande describes in her work that cultural differentiation and multiculturalism have been multiplying since the 1990s. She describes the debate about the headscarf ban as an asymmetry between the pluralized understandings of morality and religion. French society is thus seen as threatened with its morality and the change to secularism is supposed to have been this. The religious followers are thus forced to assimilate in order to gain a reputation in society only afterwards. Yolande criticises the restrictions imposed by secularisation, since politics had not previously spoken of the diversity of cultures and ethics, but had only enacted the law. It describes the homogenization of cultures and the privatization of religions in France. In her opinion, the state acted in this way, since the political decisions should have an impact on society and not on other social groups. On the other hand, these social groups present their religious symbols publicly (e.g. headscarf and kippa). On the other hand, French society today no longer presents its religious symbols, but tries to avoid them as a conspicuous feature by means of the given secularism.

"Specifically with regard to religion, we tend to interpret modern religion, adapted to secularism, as personal, individual belief or experience, and traditional, orthodox or publicly visible religious practices as either the relics of premodernity, or as the 'conspicuous signs' of postmodern identity politics, but in any case, as being on a tense footing within a modern framework. (Yolande 2018: 99).

Thus the state tries to suppress the traditions of religion in order to form a new tradition in which state and church are separated from each other.

The following chapter compares these two opinions and illuminates a broader perspective of the headscarf debate.

Comparison of both approaches

If one now goes on to compare the two comments, one notices for the first time that Asad concentrates more on the misunderstandings of politics towards religions. The French state acts only according to its incomplete understanding of religion, since it is of the opinion that the newly emerging religions and thus also cultures would endanger the traditional French culture. "Secularism is invoked to prevent two very different kinds of transgression: the perversion of politics by religious forces on the one hand, and the state's restriction of religious freedom on the other. (Asad 2006.:105). The state differentiates between the *other*

6

and *the inhabitants*, since these have other social values that are roughly incompatible with French social values. This train of thought is very biased, since people from other cultures try for the first time to arrange themselves and to integrate themselves independently. Instead, they are seen negatively and as a threat to French culture and its values. Thus, Asad demands a sensitization of the understanding of religions in order to be able to emphasize common values. This can lead to talking about the strong differences between religions in order to reach a common agreement. Laïcité represents a separate understanding of secularism, but the state only takes out the most appropriate characteristics of secularism in order to counteract the pluralisation of cultures. Yolande also takes up this point of pluralization and, like Asad, sees the behavior of politics as a counteract to the shift in the moral understanding of the French tradition. In addition, Yolande criticizes the way in which the new cultures are received, since assimilation is assumed. Through this assimilation the French society would then receive one positively. However, like secularization, assimilation is hardly possible, since socialization with the social values in another culture can never be completely removed from a human being. Assimilation can only take place over several generations, since the newer generations drop the old traditions of the parents in order to adapt to the new traditions. In conclusion, both authors take a critical view of the situation and demand that the government raise awareness of the situation. The state should not perceive a change in social values as negative, but tolerate it. Just because new publicly conspicuous traditions emerge does not mean that they endanger society or replace old traditions.

Conclusion

Based on the previous chapter, it can be concluded that the French state chose secularism as a solution for a possible alienation of culture. They transformed it into the Laïcité, while only incorporating their assessment of secularism. Thus, an important aspect of secularism was ignored: the neutrality of religions. The Laïcité particularly values the Islamic religion, since it assumes that young women are urged to wear headscarves. In this context, the conditions and possibilities of an "Islam de France" that is compatible with the values of the republic from a French point of view and, as it were, European, are discussed. However, this is opposed to the construct of a universalistically oriented, nation-independent "Islam en France". The French identity is regarded as threatened, since there is an excess of headscarf wearers in society. But to what extent culture is really threatened is not a publicly debatable political issue, since it is seen as a right-wing extremist attitude.

In my opinion, it is also quite striking that the ban on headscarves has only been limited to adolescents in school institutions. Politicians are thus trying to culturally change their socialization so that future generations will completely renounce religious symbols. I agree with the two authors of this work that the restriction of religions from politics is a wrong approach to protect social values from change. It would make more sense for the first time, as Asad describes it, to understand cultures and religions more precisely and possibly discover similarities. Thus, the other religions should be accepted, since a mixture of cultures cannot be prevented. However, one solution could be to consolidate one's own values and morals in society through educational campaigns and events. Thus, the other cultures would not be suppressed and the following generations would still stick to the traditional morality.

In conclusion, I can say from my perspective that the French identity is even more threatened by the idiosyncratic law decrees. Anyone who creates an identity for a country must feel welcome and accepted for the first time in it, after which social values and traditions are voluntarily adopted. Instead of restricting migrants with laws based on their religion, they should be given the opportunity to discover French culture on their own. The state should therefore rather invest in representing itself in an accommodating state. As Asad had described at the beginning of his commentary: "the worldly care of its population regardless of its beliefs" (Asad 2005: 94), the state should respect and esteem its citizens.

Either way, the already habitualised religious symbols can no longer be removed from people; only over generations can changes be noted.

Resources

- Asad, Talal (2006): "French secularism and the 'Islamic veil affair' (1).".
- Erlings, Esther (2018): "A Way out of Laicite - The Child's Best interests as Justification for Religious Manifestation". Cambridge: Cambridge University Press
- Yolande, Jansen (2013): "Laïcité and assimilation in the Third Republic and today". Amsterdam: Amsterdam University Press.

YOUR KNOWLEDGE HAS VALUE

- We will publish your bachelor's and
  master's thesis, essays and papers

- Your own eBook and book -
  sold worldwide in all relevant shops

- Earn money with each sale

Upload your text at www.GRIN.com
and publish for free